KU-195-404

JOHN MINGAY

INTERNAL EXILE

Selected Shorter Poems 1988-95

UNIVERSITY OF SALZBURG

SALZBURG - OXFORD - PORTLAND

1996

First published in 1996 by **Salzburg University** in its series:

SALZBURG STUDIES IN ENGLISH LITERATURE
POETIC DRAMA & POETIC THEORY
161

EDITORS: WOLFGANG GÖRTSCHACHER & JAMES HOGG

ISBN 3-7052-0055-0

INSTITUT FÜR ANGLISTIK UND AMERIKANISTIK
UNIVERSITÄT SALZBURG
A-5020 SALZBURG
AUSTRIA

© John Mingay

John Mingay is hereby identified as author of this work in accordance with Section 77 of the Copyright, Designs and Patents Act 1988.

Distributed by
Drake International Services
Market House, Market Place,
Deddington OXFORD OX15 0SF
England
Fax N°: 01869 338310

SILENCE WITH TEETH

an introduction to the poetry of John Mingay by Norman Jope

There are modernists and there are post-modernists. There are also, arguably, writers who can be described as presentists. Categories are often hateful, but it may make sense to describe the poetry of John Mingay as **momentist**. That does not exhaust its resources in any way - but it is probably fair to say that Mingay's best, and most characteristic work, is written in the interstices of experience. It is not concerned with the process of events, as much as stepping back from events, to escape into a deeper reality.

Some readers have a problem with poetry that is not demonstrably 'about' something - it's even the kind of thing that can feature on rejection slips. Mingay's work is often evasive of theme, and rarely deals in story lines - indeed, it is possible that Mingay is less successful when he uses them. That's not a weakness - with so many writers around, we can all afford to specialise. And we learn, in time, that we do certain things well, and that others do different things well - completeness is for the mass of us. To argue otherwise would be like claiming that Tommy Steele was a better singer than Nick Drake, because Nick Drake couldn't tap-dance (at least, if he did, he kept it quiet). That's not meant as a comparison, although readers may guess my preference - it's simply meant to indicate the meaninglessness of such comparisons.

Many of the poems in this collection, therefore, are to do with pauses - the aftermaths of events, the timeless points at which they are about to happen. A perfect example is *itinerance* - a remarkably stripped and simple piece, in which the writer is sitting on a bench in Bishop Auckland - nothing more than that, he's meeting no-one, doing nothing, simply smoking a cigarette (the cigarette functions as an image of repose in several pieces, and should not be misconstrued as cancer stick). Mingay writes of 'another day/another town//Thursday's town//so many miles/from Monday' So what's this about? What does it *mean*? To ward off the hyenas, I will interpret it as an image of a pause from time, not a final resting-place but an indication of the void behind time's passage. Another piece, *Cigarette*, denotes a similar point of pause, in which 'time is marked by the silence/of its scattering'.. Mingay's conceit, (in the positive sense), is that the act of writing a poem allows both writer and reader to step out of time, only in so **many words** - a moment without duration is expanded, to admit the thoughts that would otherwise pass unvoiced. Unusually, it takes longer to read one of Mingay's poems, on the whole, than to act it out.

Mingay is as attracted to borderlines, and regions of transition, as he is to the magic of particular moments - each moment, of course, being another sort of borderline. He is concerned with transitional points on the clock, and on the calendar - dawn, dusk, spring, autumn. For example, one of the first pieces in the collection is entitled *The Crepuscular Sought* - the 'crepuscular' being defined as that which 'is known only as something/held within the darkness coming'. In *Sandflies*, he notes 'The distant tide/like/a motionless clock' - in the summer twilight, the sandflies parallel the hypnogogic flashes that accompany the passage into sleep. On the other hand, however, Mingay celebrates the dawn - in *whore of the dawn*, it/she is described as 'the teeth/of tomorrow to come' and in *first light*, the dawn is pinned down as a moment cast in sudden sharp relief, 'this day/inherited/from a silhouetted world'.

Sometimes, the twilight can be a human one - in *Drawing In*, an old man sitting on a bench, in the rain, silently celebrates 'a life filled full/of memorable whispers that echo/even now as he waits wet-through for dusk'. His life has been unexceptional - he still wears his demob raincoat, forty years later. But, as Maeterlinck and others have pointed out, there can be more drama, more heroism in the quiet moments of our lives than in the throes of action. Who can say what is more or less alive, in any case? The convention is that life resides in movement, but it is also possible that it resides, in a more essential sense, in the purer passage of time. And, arguably, it is by stripping away the biography, the experience, that one can arrive at the real, at least as surely as from the opposite direction.

Mingay's **via negativa** reminds me of a late poem by Gunnar Ekelöf, *Xoanon*. It concerns the slow stripping of a Byzantine icon - the elaborate figure of the Madonna is whittled out of existence, to reveal the wooden base behind it, the knot of the branch protruding into the grain. The delirium of overload, of the hyperdelic richness of a writer like Steve Sneyd or Peter Redgrove, can achieve a similar effect, like passages of jazz-rock, say mid-period Magma, that can move so fast they almost seem to stand still (this conjures up a picture of Magma's drummer Christian Vander eight years ago at the Bloomsbury Theatre, drumming at such a speed that there appeared to be no movement, in the end, at all, just **sound**). Mingay's approach, as with a comparable writer Colin Oliver, is otherwise - a luminous emptiness is revealed, by the paring away of events, the isolation of moments and their contents.

The result of this can only be spiritual, and there are many signs in this book that Mingay does not reject such a reading - at one point, for example, he alludes to the watercourse way of Tao, and one could interpret much of his work as a search for the Yin, in the face of the overpowering and insistent demands of the Yang. But his spirituality is humble, and refuses, on the whole, to inflate itself into myth. It is a sense, rather, of a reality so vast, so mysterious, so obscure, that (*Further In*) 'no words can carry/a sufficiency to know'. It is a world in which experiences overload, to the point where they must be sloughed at intervals - for example, in *vacuum*, they are seen as rust, a pile of dust, or 'fallow acres/of mounting fragments'. Exhaustion is almost welcomed by Mingay as (paradoxically) the stimulus to escape into a more numinal reality.

So what is the **use** of this, assuming there can be one? Mingay's work can help us still the flow, to step outside the rush of events that engulfs us daily, that is stimulated, with increasing desperation, by our hunger for experience and an economy that feeds on it. This has nothing to do with escapism, but much to do with escape - Mingay seems to imply that it is at the quietest points, sometimes, that we live most vividly. At the very least, it is a way of slowing time, of making our brief lives last a little longer.

Mingay doesn't always stick to single moments, although, even then, his poems tend to deal with the analysis of situations, rather than the depiction of events. One memorable example is *One-Zero-Three*, occasioned by the Lockerbie bombing - it doesn't attempt to describe the disaster, but skilfully talks around it, by addressing it via a beloved witness. The poem is as much about the difficulty of framing human experience in terms of truth, or answers, as it is about compassion both for the victims of the bombing and the addressed observer - 'But there are no real answers/if from an answer you expect a truth'. This kind of empiricism is typical of Mingay sometimes, an empirical approach can be a cue for arrogance, in the way that Dr Johnson refuted Berkeley's theories by stubbing a toe on a rock, or some critics dismiss any poetry of spiritual reference as 'irrelevant' (or even, O hammerblow of hammerblows, 'pretentious') but Mingay's tentative approach to reality is not in the least bit dismissive. If it were so, of course, then it would contradict itself.

Compassion and modesty go hand in hand in many of the better pieces. At times, the sheer overload of the world, its barrage of words and signs, of clichés and postures, inclines him to a hint of misanthropy, as in *Mindless After The Monkey* - here, his pub companions have 'allowed the monkey/to steal their thoughts,/what thoughts there were to steal'. This is not **really** misanthropy, however, as much as a sign of the exhaustion, the sense of overload, that can be so creative in other pieces. It is generally outweighed by the compassionate pieces, particularly those addressed to a partner or the writer's baby. As a result of the chronological ordering of the book, the child begins to surface about two-thirds of the way through, and his growth in the womb, and triumphant arrival, forms an effective coda. From a length of 4.5 cm - the title of one piece, which describes him, most simply, as 'in there/you/waiting/growing' the child becomes 'the sun/held aloft/and delivered... smeared/with journey's blood' in the final piece, *family*. In more arrogant hands, the sun/son link could have come across as cliché - but here, the honest sense of celebration stops this happening.

Mingay offers us a humanist approach, therefore, without the baggage of 'realism' or 'relevance' - moreover, he is a writer in possession of a quiet skill. It is notable, for this reader, how the skill becomes most evident when the writing is simplest - some of the longer, more elaborate pieces falter, and drift, in comparison with shorter poems like *itinerance*, *Cigarette*, and the poem written in the aftermath of poetry that goes under the title of *Cracked* - 'I have said my piece/and no longer want to speak;/muteness, like a swan's.' At the moment, certainly, there appears to be a fascinating tension in contemporary free-press (as opposed to small-press!) poetry, between writers who deal in overload, to attempt to meet the cavalcade of late C20 mediated reality head on (sometimes reflecting it beyond reductible meaning, as with many of the linguistically-innovative poetries associated with anthologies like *Floating Capital and Out of Everywhere*) and writers like Mingay, Oliver and others, who tend to, retreat from the overload in order to acquire a stable standpoint. Most writers currently active oscillate between the poles of 'richness' and 'simplicity', between, perhaps, the Tantric and the Vedantic - there's no right or wrong to the dichotomy, and anyone who says so is attempting to deprive the reader of a total picture.

More than ever, it has to be recognized that none of us writers will complete the picture by ourselves - it is the totality of writing that will do so, and we can only even **read** a tiny portion, hardly even a valid sample. This is a strong collection, generally, because Mingay has found his angle - probably more and more surely, as the collection progresses - and, in so doing, he indicates to all of us the possibilities of a simpler, deeper, richer life. Revolving around a core vocabulary which is almost Platonic in its elemental emphasis, and laudable for its honesty, persistence and vigilance, Mingay's poetry is a clear case of the 'silence with teeth' he describes. It travels from its moments of enactment, quiet as a buried watercourse - however, when it surfaces, the results refresh and quench the thirst.

Contents

viii

x

Gratitude is extended to the editors of the following magazines and presses in whose publications poems in this collection first appeared:

Acumen, Anthem, Apparitions Press, ASWELLas, Cadmium Blue Literary Journal, Contraflow, Day by Day, Good Society Review, Headlock, Lung Gom Press, Memes, Nineties Poetry, Nutshell, Odyssey, Ore, Ostinato, Paladin, Psychopoetica, Ramraid Extraordinaire, Raunchland Publications, Sepia, Songs, Stride, Tees Valley Writer, 10th Muse, Terrible Work, Understanding, Wurdz Publications.

For Hélène & Boris

"Of course, a certain optimism is not my speciality." (Albert Camus)

Decadent Harvest.

"An age that melts in unperceiv'd decay,
And glides in modest innocence away."

(Samuel Johnson.)

Through these rain-washed streets
seep so many signs of
before, of a time when
friends walked side by side,
each knowing of the other
as no other could, understanding
the other as no other
could, familiar and touched by
similar passions; the pulsing of
their blood in unison like
the chanting of a choir,

Not celestial but of this
earth, this land where men
are men and nothing more,
nothing as grand as gods
nor as small as slaves;
just men; sons of mothers
who have bitten at life
as though to have tasted
its pleasures, taken its crop
and sown more seed, then
waited for the harvest again;
and even now, through the

Cracking tar, their echoing words
can be heard, sensed as
warning of the way things
are and will come to
be so soon, so grey,
flattened by the decay that
we leave behind; no seed
now that grows free from
disease, only the poxed and
peccant prick to stab at
the slit, to carry the
future no further; no father,

no mother, just unsigned space

That churns its emptiness as
though to make something from
nothing while knowing no need
for knowing another; yet, no brother
is safe in walking alone,
walking these streets of
rain-washed tar, these streets
where, in time, the echoes
will diminish as the harvest
is reaped no more and
as all that was known
becomes lost in the scrub,
lost without mention nor mourning,
lost, never to breathe again.

revealing the curve

billowing in the wind
scattered finery
    like thoughts
    fragile
      thoughts
    fleeting

lace of summer's hem
         hers
        perfumed
pervading scent
    reminiscent
forcing each thought
       to plunge

deep into before
      breaching
memory's walls
       to the core
to the embryo
of the dream

dreamt in this summer's
        haze
        heat
      heat-haze
like an illusion
of the sun

a mirage
    in
a desert of loneliness
her song
  a song of
       togetherness
         again

together with silk
  against softest skin
wrapping
clinging

revealing the curve
the swelling
that dresses as hope

Aftermath

*

... And we watched the storm-clouds gather,
                        clouds so furious
as to be unaware of their trail
        and unaware of the destruction
they were leaving behind;

A blooded world hacked at by daggers;

Her dagger, my dagger:

*

She touched, I touched, together we touched,
both a part of the aftermath;

Our hands searched and scored marks
in each other's flesh, animal-like,
until, amid the rubble, there was screaming pain,
                        survival's pain,
screaming in the hope that time would disperse;

As though time was the enemy,
                time to kill,
so slow though so sudden the featureless face,
the dozen to be swept in silent passage,
the pallid circle that brought closer our deaths:

*

But this dream,
        if a dream it was,
only became apparent when, at last, her touch
was softened, was subdued by dew
that dripped in the half-light
                half-way haze
of morning's welcoming haar from which
silhouettes emerged as friends:

*

The first, Abas, looked at himself writhing,
lizard-like, and just for laughing, for mocking
the corn with an uncontrollable contempt;

He came out from the shade,
                from under the stone and met the light
as though attempting, with remorse,
to forget the past;

He came to join us, hissing, his licking tongue
tongueing a word;

'Friends';
And, with this, the moment seemed infinite
as though time had finally dispersed, diffused
while, in the sky, something moved, fleetingly seen:

*

Soaring bird,
    steel bird, wings open wide upon thermals,
upon the terminal illusion of profile;

Presence:

*

Abas from lizard switched to ox, expiring
in the brilliance by obelisks held,
held as if to hold the storm,
to calm the storm, to scatter the clouds,
and as though to allow another to come,
                another to replace
        the first one lost,
                another silhouette
        as friend;

This friend we watched come from the heart,
                from the centre
of the shadow, speaking his name, while feeling
we should already have known;

Viracocha:

*

Viracocha, the creator god,
            a demi-god who, from earth and sky,
made the darkened world, and who decided this world
should be sown with people;

                  Stone people,
                  giant people,
                        people who were soon
to cause him grief, to come to
            grief under a swelling ocean
that swallowed all but two;

East and West;

The East and West from where our storm-clouds came,
from where Viracocha came, all so briefly to emerge
before to become but a memory once more:

*

She cried a tear
that turned to crystal:

*

Yet, even with his passing, the cavalcade continued,
resounding with the music of distant wind
and with the echoing suck as the vacuum was filled,
                        the vacuum that was
      the morning's welcoming haar,
a half-light
      half-way haze:

*

We coaxed and egged until Mortimar appeared,
unwilling as he was to relinquish the shade;

Two heads,
two mouths,
a schizoid monster, man of the twilight,
a howling wolf who bathed in the moon, swearing
demise upon any who dared, any as foolish

as to cross his path;

A route that once had taken him southwards,
down the spine to find Timia,
            to find the gorge
where Tuareg boys stand, shading themselves
under gnarled bark mapped out like the centuries,
            mapped out like ochre flesh
awaiting the sands that spread starvation;

This schizoid monster came forward, mouths open,
ready to speak in two tongues together;

'The addax was my brother':

*

Another crystal tear
marked a line down her cheek:

*

She looked, I looked, together we looked,
both a part of the aftermath,
both a part of the emptiness left,
            left with nothing
when the silhouettes ceased to emerge
and when the blooded world was left to bleed:

*

The storm-clouds then
dispersed like hours;

Our daggers the dirks that dug.

*

The Crepuscular Sought

Cradle eyes, puncturing,
loath to blink,
scouring the plain
in hopeful gaze,
        as gauze-misted,
hoisted in the sight-path
that scans the flight-path
        of the incoming night,
scented with summer's waiting
and ringing with angels' whispers;

Sharp to focus, fixedly,
on even a speck,
a seagull astray
in snow-hung skies,
        perhaps disguise,
for the object sought
wears no carnation
        nor old school tie,
it is known only as something
held within the darkness coming.

come

membraned fingers
stretch cold in the haar,
needle-like,
functionless
but to point out the sun;

and nails fail to cipher.

Drawing In

Old man waits with wasted eyes,
hands on stick as though stuck,
as though bench-bound in an
eloquent silence as he scrapes
up an image to replace
or to reproduce the image lost;

His de-mob gabardine stained,
soiled by elements through time,
though shrouding him still in comfort,
coddling him still as though wrapped
in the warm fleshy arms of the mother
he knew so well, so many years gone;

Listening, he hears a world,
a new world that, for him, has been
left unseen, un-lived-in but for
the square foot of peeling timber
that suffices as a throne for this
king of darkness, dead though breathing;

Yet, in his kingdom, the darkness
isn't blackness, rather it is
spangled with the radiance of
a life fulfilled, a life filled full
of memorable whispers that echo
even now as he waits wet-through for dusk.

clearest

from the outside
looking in,
seeing with a clarity
untainted by caprice,
untinted by rose
that would otherwise cloud
as though to
captivate judgement
in sentiment's ring;
a bond that binds
the sight to see
with nothing of the nuance
the stranger sees,
and with little
of the laughter
his leaving leaves
having seen the scene
without wetted eyes.

gripped

the coil
wraps
holes
and steals
with the devil
for a bedfellow

with a whore to lick
though no luck
herein

no life to leave
but for the life
long given
as though in glorious
trenches
where the battle begun
recommences

where the desolate coil
unwinds
unfelt
and unused
with a grape
gripped between the teeth

with a sun
folding

though no holding
no holding
no holds barred

barren
this clay
baked

first light

time and seed
lightly waxed
of water born

as in a name of earth
removed
blessed so that death
could see the sun

see the stone
of sun and seed
watered and kissed

gathered

till morning
called this name
and conceived again

and bore a fruit of harvest
speckled
spotted with white
and children's loss

children's years
of fear afraid
and night enough

night enough to dream

the whore beyond

hungered,
sharp-set, starved;
eyes seek more
than these canyons of brick
and currents of black;

skin softens
at the thought
of beyond the lines of signs
that signal
the limits of this lime-twig lure;

but unreachable,
intangible;
only its scent
occasionally blown
as though a prick-teasing whore.

crocodile

so summer
    summer eyes drip
    golden eyes
    crying eyes
the link between
      bitten
      umbilical shattered
by pretence
    presumption

no sooner said than the saying
sinks as slivers of scorn
      and the crying of summer
        begins again so summer
          again
          again

          again the pulse
          a tic
          a twitch
          a lash trembles

        then gathers the tear

the one to burn

her sandalwood cheeks blush
with the beat of conscience
with the heat of coloured clouds
acrid clouds

understandable eyes
hands
jealous gestures

simply black with light
like paper exposed to the sun

slow to turn
to blink
to blind
to clasp

her grasp on reality slipping
as she asks the invisible
in a scrambled voice
why she
above all others
must be the one to burn

to turn
like the sun

and be blinded
without jury
for her jealousy
gestured

162/XX/VI/LIIIVIII

whispering
'She's gone!'

bruised hands

ears forget the answers
forget everything
forget the fingers

skin
numb

another blood

and you
you wanted the skin
numb

you wanted to wash the blood

wanted
and
asked

wild as the devil
but often as divided
as paper figures

frustrated

cut

because

it's hard to explain;

coming in,
going out,

people sit,
sharp,
people that lived there
just once,

still thinking,

kept thinking
because of the answers,

because of the angels.

whore of the dawn

her rustling words
    burnt with yellow

her lips like time
    and settled seeds

she a mother
    to the rising sigh

she the teeth
    of tomorrow to come

these elephants

I could make sounds
like the hiss
of sour grapes
deflating,
yet, still, these elephants,
so eloquent
as to pass bull
as gospel,
would hear nothing
but the tune
of their mouths
farting in the wind.

the 'four gentlemen'

* * *

at Shisendo
the immortal poet
strokes an orchid

knowing himself noble

though reluctant
to spread the scent

* * *

one of seven
of the bamboo grove

this sage's integrity
solid

strong

yet flexible

* * *

as plum blossom
from pink to white

the actor changes

a weeping old man
becomes
Mikenjaku

* * *

modest emperor
reclusive
clutches a chrysanthemum

the oppression

he commands
inherited

* * *

Cathedral

Beating heart
before evensong;

Metal amidst masonry
as old as the canyon
cleft to flow.

Durham 9th August 1988

the inimitable face of the charade

behind eyes that have seen solid walls fall
images surge with the weight of terror
tearing at the softness of thoughts
to create fears amongst the chaos of
deadened branches hanging hung

and the beasts come

animals gorging themselves on
the sinewed children of the cross
like anglicans in a ruse whose whim
whose caprice is a cud of crying flesh
cold though pulsing still

behind eyes that have seen nothing but dirt
visions haunt each second of time
in a merciless contortion of truths
half-chewed half-told half-found though
truths believed in for want of belief

wont waters to drown in

the vision of baptism witnessed by spectres
staring with death's inimitable face
expressionless other than a hint of
suffering like sediment in a river running
with indifference running without moving

behind eyes that have seen the lost return
icons no longer hold their pose each having
become a juggler an acrobat a clown in the
circus of saints fallen fallen foul
frightened now as the canvas flutters

ill-wind oblivious to dawn

the terror reigns through night and day
through rains and sun salt-rubbed wounds
thorn scratches seeping with the blood

of doubt and disloyal deception to make
history no more than part of the charade

even the sacred cow is raped

litter scatters on the heavy nose of the morning rush
the wind retards each step in a well-worn path
a sleep-eyed sun rests sunk so low as to be nothing but light
shadows stretch as though each id lives as a tarmac giant
the weight of walls presses in to stifle to trap
and somewhere beyond even the horizon is choking a cough

even the sacred cow is raped

in the sight-line

she turns and waves
then
only her back is seen

fading

others cross the sight-line
as though to obstruct
any lasting memory

as always

always others
who got in the way
who helped the end along

unknowingly

even   song

whistles, cars,

breath, clock,

a   scream.

fathomless, close to the edge

in the quest for quietude
we were drawn
to where centuries' walls
stood, still, silent,
guarding the peace
of the princes' landscape's edge.

we came,
we saw,
and we were conquered,
captured in the creases
of an aging flesh,
a skin of fructuous stretching,

a covering to absorb
heaven's tears, softly falling,
silent in submission
to the whims of descent,
silent in submission
while the earth drew the pain.

we came,
we saw,
and we knew,
we could sense that time,
racing elsewhere,
was fathomless, here, close to the edge.

Barnard Castle
25th September 1988

72

Spitting ochre
of autumn light.

Crisp underfoot,
leaves dying, dead.

Weathered timbers
as charcoal pins.

Hung overhead,
boughs slumber bare.

Coldness seeping,
though not yet full.

Hamsterley's boles,
caught, snatched by time.

after a painting
by Paul Dillon

Mindless After The Monkey

I could almost have wept for them
finding them as they were,
seemingly dead but breathing,
going through the motions,
giving the impression of being
feeling, thinking, creatures of this earth,

I could almost have cut the air,
so heavy laden with futility,
using only a word for a knife,
and not even a sharp word,
any, even one blunted by cliche,
even one of their own,

I could almost have felt pity
had it not been for the fact
that they themselves were their own burden,
they themselves had allowed the monkey
to steal their thoughts,
what thoughts there were to steal.

submerged tenth

sky
sky-blue

gulls
  screeching
  swooping
  seeking
the unsuspecting

  sentenced
without trial
to be plucked at dawn

     from dawn
     to dusk

  unrelenting
  unrepenting
  executioners
      scour
    the waves

hungry eyes
  beady eyes

  blind to the fall
    to all
but the silver
  the scales

  for the moment
unevenly balanced

  redress to come

icon

praise for
the father
of all
creation;
he who is
mysterious,
yet is known
to all.
of crown-like light   praise for
                             the
                             craftsman
luminous nimbus   who moulded
siren of   this world;
diversion and   this sphere
enticement;   once pure,
mother of all,   now shamed
born herself of   by man.
unconscious   praise for
waters;   the planner
an unknown   who now
damsel loved.   feels
                             the pain.

her hand
clutches the tool
of silent conversation.

Old Dogs - Old Tricks

The path is narrow,
Hedged-in, hemmed-in,
With acres spreading beyond,
Unseen, unexplored;

Eyes forward,
Onward,
And long teeth bared to the wind
In resolute, satisfied smiles;

Old dogs,
Unwilling to learn new tricks,
Sniff at the familiar scents
Laid down through centuries along the track;

Eyes forward,
Onward,
Only to reach where others have been,
Where others have watched the torch splutter and die;

Lack of air,
Fresh air,
But safe in the stifling coldness
Of passionless pandering;

Eyes forward,
Onward,
Old dogs leashed by faceless masters
Who help the lie to breathe;

This lie, this myth,
Makes a pariah of each prophet
Who strays beyond the hedge
Into the acres of fertile terrain;

Eyes forward,
Onward,
The pariah-dog learns new tricks,
The pariah-dog pisses elsewhere.

Quartet

December To Come

Delicate mosaic of merging boughs' summer shroud;
Beneath, in a sun-kissed harmony, lovers lie entwined;

Their story much as mine, much as ours;
Eyes that found eyes
And found hearts within to love.

Remembered

Darkened departure,
Summer remembered;

Monfrid sucks his forefinger
Then tests the wind;

Westerly;

Laced with balm
From the bole of pine;

He remembers her face
Still soft from the first found kiss beneath the boughs.

Embers

'My body shook like a volcano erupting,
Spitting embers into a far from virgin sky;

Her heart was open, mine searching,
Hoping to find a knowing lost;

The setting of cement for the delicate mosaic
Set to crumble to dust.'

December At Last

Their story much as mine, much as ours;
Passing, fleeting, stolen;

The chill of December
Brought a bareness to the boughs;

Persuaded,
Monfrid returned to another summer's eyes.

Ours

No more a pricking briar,
Soft now,
Safe;

Half-lived,
But breathing still,
Breathing in this moment
That is a moment before;

The breathlessness
Of the heat
Gone;

Coolness;

Sucking in
The new-found;

The idea
Of anything else
Only restlessness;

Ritual-weariness;

But this hour,
Ours,
Is an hour
That will lead to another;

And,
Even then,
Again.

One-Zero-Three

You laugh and find the day sleeping,
    sombre,
    tied up in a tangle of pain;
Your eyes are my eyes, our eyes,
    eyes of disbelief
    with the incredible light of night
    still flashing, still burning,
    searing through perception
    as though to challenge sight;
You see the expected star
    come unexpectedly as fire, falling,
    fragmented and scattered
    like ashes over a sea;
Your heart sinks, you feel it sink
    and hear its words whispered within
    like a sigh, like a secret
    whispering your name throughout time:

*

You trace the light as though at least
    to give it the chance of persuading you
    the characters of its realm are real;
But you remain unconvinced,
    unable to take in these names,
    unable to allow these names to enter
    and be your guides;
Though within, you can still hear the whispers
    of your own name being sighed
    as a secret;
And your eyes reflect your heart:

*

Your thoughts, I have found,
    are thoughts drenched in a purity
    that can still wonder about destruction
    and that can question, in the face of love,
    as to why so many must perish
    for the sake of a mythical speed;
And your eyes, I have found,

are the eyes of a child who can watch
without recourse to condemnation
and who can sense the sublime
without falling headlong
into the fathomless well
of understanding sought;
But above all, I have found your heart
is a heart that is open,
welcoming all to rest and find comfort
in the delicate folds of its sun-shaded,
pain-shaded warmth of wisdom,
wise to the ways of the world:

*

You hold the debris of a dream in your hands,
a nightmare wherein nothing was known,
nothing was concluded
nor certain except grief;
You examine it, turn it and feel the horror
of an everlasting second
that left only the faintest noise,
an unfinished noise
from which to surmise a cause;
You laugh and find the day sleeping,
sombre,
tied up in a tangle of pain;
And the mangled remains
lie scattered from west to east,
while from both horizons
comes the murmuring
of the advancing crowd, as yet unseen,
scavenging,
soon to be witness
with morbid delight drooling from lips:

*

But the fire dies
and there is silence, all-embracing,
songless, birdless, motionless, awestruck,
silence in which the faintest, unfinished
noise is given an end;
Yet you are no stranger to this silence

for there is nothing black
about the final drawn breath;
The only blackness is reserved
for the lurking shadows
that shroud the robbers
who scrape each limb bony-clean;
Though even then the night is hardly as dark
as to hide their ugly hands,
for, despite the dying fire,
there is still the incredible light,
flashing, burning, searing:

*

There was more than simple fate involved
in the unexpected fire that fell,
but in realizing this
you open up ever-fresher doubts;
The why and how are added to
by the question of who?
Unknown faces so many miles away,
faces that your eyes, our eyes,
have never seen,
nor will ever see;
These faces laugh, not with disbelief
but with satisfaction at having scored,
at having used surprise
to down the bird and scatter
the contents of its heaving belly;
And their eyes reflect only flame:

*

The tangle of pain tightens all the more
with the news that the threat was known;
You spit with fury at the paper-chase
that led the unexpecting into the forest
and left them there, unknowing and unaware;
You wonder why the forest is so dark
when each tree bears an unlit torch;
But there are no real answers
if from an answer you expect a truth;
There is only the senseless defence
that to have told

would have meant telling and telling again;
A senselessness to preserve the mythical speed
and to allow the umbilical to stretch:

*

You laugh and find another day sleeping
with only the sound of saws
rasping at the skeletal remains;
Soon all will be forgotten,
the ruins razed, the crater filled,
the wounds healed, the wreckage found,
and the lessons learnt;
But will it ever be forgotten enough
to lose the memory?
Will the razing of the ruins
not leave a gap as reminder?
Will the wounds ever heal
so as to leave no trace on flesh or heart?
Will every piece of debris ever be found?
And will the lessons learnt
ever have any bearing on the incessant race?
These are your questions,
each of them asked in the face of love,
each of them asked with a whispered sigh:

*

And as you carry away the final bone
I can see that your limbs are heavy,
but also that your heart is heavier still;
There is, as there always will be,
that reflection in your eyes,
nothing as melodramatic as tears
or banshee wailing,
just a simple compassion
compounded by confusion;
You have laughed and found and seen,
you have traced and held and spat,
and you have wondered about the bird downed
and about so much else,
so much so your face is a landscape
mapped by both caresses and blows,
moulded into a terrain

that holds history as a friend;
Your face is my face, our face,
a face that turns a cheek
time and time again.

*

Sandflies

As I reach out into the crumbling dusk
there is a sense of peace
in knowing the night-silence is to come.

Your voice
        is speechless
               in this silence.

My hand, with its five fingers, touches
air sapped by the scorching sun of day
and drags its nails through the dryness.

My eyes
       absorb you
             through the dimness.

Desperately I will the taciturn-hours
with their secret-like emptiness
to chase what remains of the arid light.

Then the night-silence
           arrives
              at last.

And like a hunted man, I search the darkest,
quietest corner to wait and listen
for your footsteps, muted, hardly heard.

The sand
       barely disturbed
             by each step.

With nothing said, speechless still,
we watch the sandflies jump
and feel the softness of the darkness.

We shroud
       ourselves
             in its cambric hours.

The distant tide
　　　like
　　　　a motionless clock.

now with the empty snow

half-hidden
   by a thick veil of flowers
like clouds,
like running water in the wind,
she sings;

her face,
dry and withered
       yet shining blood-red,
beautiful;

her song like a poem,
      a storm,
    a memory of warmth;

      summer and sun,
a skin caressed.

In The Garden of Eyes

Dead men's eyes like cracked, black stones,
like poisonous nights that fill this garden with intent;
insistent eyes that take hold, half-seen, of dreams
and scenes to look within for the thought conceived;
their landscape but a blackness,
a field of flapping, unfamiliar trees;
thick wood,
dark wood like moving cloud caught on the tongue;
these eyes, neither smooth nor sharp, are heavy,
are ready to sleep the sleep of the few,
a sleep obscured by the square of time;
and this garden is like a hell without escape;

no sooner is the sun
than the sun is absorbed:

*

I watch these eyes watching
and wonder when the watching will cease;
their menacing stare is full of a petrification
as cold and as solid as granite gravestones
windswept from the west;
and I am caught like the moving cloud,
but not upon the tongue,
for their tongues are as silent as death's own song;
their tongues are like ice,
unmelting,
reticent;
only occasionally is there a partial thaw
that allows something of their souls to be aired;

but no sooner aired
than shrouded again:

*

In these poisonous nights I am like any other,
no longer one but one of many, the many who are held
behind the bars within this garden;
and this hellish garden is like any other,

no longer one but one of many, the many that hold
the flesh till the sap-like blood is squeezed from it
as though an orange in being forced to give up its juice;
and these trees are like any others,
no longer unique in being unfamiliar, but unfamiliar
all the same,
as unfamiliar as a kiss laced with love to this child;

and no sooner the child
than the child is a man:

*

I watch these eyes of blackened stone crack open like eggs
to reveal, not young but, an emptiness;
soullessness;
their years of stark regret and repressed desires
finally too much to withhold,
too much to dam;
and the emptiness is all that can be expected;
and the emptiness is only a reflection;
and the reflection is only another link in the chain
of emptinesses repeated time and again;
time is their millstone, their cross, their burden,
their shackles of shame at being stone-like and blind;

no sooner is the soul
than the soullessness is seen:

*

Each bough wails as the wind wakes and flails
with its frozen hands sweeping from the west;
this wailing stirs something within me
as though to take hold and torture
whatever there is of a soul remaining
after so long in the garden with the eyes watching;
this wailing is the wailing of a mother
cradling her dead child when all around has been destroyed;
this wailing is mine, wailed by the trees
in surrogacy for my own silent mouth;
my muteness contains everything of before,
a history unspoken yet heard by all who have heard
the birdless skies sigh in their lonely vastness;

but no sooner my silence
than my silence is broken:

*

My lips bleed with the speed of speaking these words,
words that have only previously echoed within;
one word in particular,
one word that leads to others as parts of the same,
parts of this soul, this flesh, this mind;
I;
so seldom used, so often entombed
in a lexicon that allowed the garden to be a secret,
a suffered secret until the time was right;
and that time is now,
now that the child is man,
now that the trees have been uprooted and parted
to provide a route to find eyes beyond;

and no sooner found
than found with tears:

*

But her tears and her kisses are laced with love,
her weeping weighed not with sadness but with completion;
together we have escaped our separate gardens;
together we have escaped the staring eyes;
together we have forced our way between the trees
to meet on common ground, on sacred ground, on safe ground,
a sanctuary of sorts,
a nest in which to repair our wings
for the next inevitable flight;
and yet we know we are not alone, we are not unique;
we are only two of many, the many who have broken free
from behind the bars of their own gardens of eyes;

but no sooner together
than the union is tried:

*

Other eyes, equally akin to cracked, black stones,
judging and sentencing before the crimeless crime

has even been committed;
judging and sentencing with all the righteousness
of a god-kissed ass;
their holiness unholy, their values fragile,
formed by a quarterless hammer of fear;
fathomless;
fixed vision, skyward, in the hope of salvation
in return for preventing the sinless sin
from being committed;
contrite;
yet we can see through them as though gossamer,
as though glass;

and no sooner sentenced
than freed to fly:

*

And now our garden we wait to fill,
not with unfamiliar, flapping trees, but with flowers;
and we wait to watch,
not with eyes like cracked, black stones, but of love;
and we wait for the screams,
not of pain, but of pleasure,
not of wanting, but of having,
not of fear, but of comfort;
and our sleep will not be slept
until the square of time no longer obscures;
our sleep will only be slept when our garden
is empty again and the screams are but echoes of the past;

no sooner heard
than heard no more.

* * *

arousal

in stripeless purdah,
hemp-bound and innominate -

provoking prurience
in the gapers and gogglers,
the oglers and eyers,
huddled,
held-breathed,
waiting in suspense,
tense -

a body?
head too big, too flat -
hatted?
shoulders too narrow, too straight -
then, what?

breaths held,
presumptions aroused -

after Henry Moore's 'Crowd looking at a tied-up Object' (1942)

Climbing

The screaming Abelam rips her heart out
and pleads to be mother
while murdered words beat from within,
                    beat from beneath,
            seeping then slitting,
            scarring,
                    the initiation begins...

            Barren no longer,
                    no longer girl,
now woman with life to meet life to make life,
                            to bear...

            I ask her for a hair,
a single strand upon which to climb
                    towards knowing;
                    her eyes say, "take";
                            she is happy in knowing
                            all she knows
                    despite the worshipped yam
            and the six seedless moons...

            I climb the strand
                    of her shorn innocence
                    and find the sky
boiling with the ochre smeared on a child,
burning with the embers that have set a soul free...

            But my own still seeks,
                    still searches,
                            still scavenges for a love;
the promised warmth of earth and mud,
            whether the Asmat mud of mourning
            or the quick-rising earth
                    the Bunlap find...

            I climb ever higher
                            until the strand tapers
and becomes an invisible tree scented with life,
its leaves crisp to the touch
                    yet unseen,

its bark damp with escaping sap;
tasting a wetted finger I come to know
what the Abelam knows...

Out of twelve
only six are seedless moons,
and from the seventh the seed will flow again
to fill her full
and repair her sundered heart...

Estuary Desk

Like veins,
endless veins of tubing, of piping,
occasionally hiccupping,
rising into unceremonious arches
that stand starkly against the treeless horizon
of a wetland desert;

Like veins,
running, not beneath but, across the flesh
of this broken landscape,
this desolate, fiery, smoky scene
from where seals have been exiled
to cling at the edge;

Like veins,
carrying, not blood but, the gases needed
to feed the furnaces,
these infernal, insatiable fires
that warm the near-birdless skies
but for scavenging gulls and crows;

In pain,
amidst it all, I travel eastward
wrapped in a cacoon,
in a bogied sheath, looking for man
but seeing only his marks left
like schoolboy carvings on an estuary desk;

In pain,
amidst it all, I travel seaward
wondering how, or even if this can be a part
of the general scheme of things,
if this can be a part of the intended path
when our feet are so close to the ground;

In pain.
amidst it all, I travel outward
knowing that even my own path
is part of the cautionless carving,
part of the life-line feeding the furnaces,
but my mouth is too small to complain.

Screw

His hope
crossed the ring
of her eye
like a kissing,
splashing,
sloppy fool
flushed with the breathing
of a better god;

But this hope was like
the beginning rain,
too quick
to make the day
laugh or scream;

Though it could
simply have been
a naked tongue
hanging free,
flat flesh,
honoured
like the infant
loved and in love,
left with nothing
but milk;

But still,
he promised her
anything there was
to be had,
and would have tried
to imagine happiness
had it struck him
to suppose it
a possible course;

And, in parallel,
her hand,
pretending carelessness,
couldn't hide her soul,
so tender

though little dreamt of
in sleep
or when the winds
of wonder woke;

So much so,
she found
the day wouldn't fit
despite his whispers
of the breaking breath
of death
and of a better god
to be praised.

cloister whispers

speaking tongues,
  forked tongues
      cutting the air
      with transparent words,

each laced,
      laden with a hundred years
      of futile tears
      wept within.

itinerance

as the smoke
from another cigarette
drifts

I sit
bench-bound

thankful
for this near-silent
sanctuary

this island
in a day
in a town

another day
another town

Thursday's town

so many miles
from Monday

Bishops' Palace Gardens
Bishop Auckland
17th March 1989

as the cry of a childless father

the dam bursts and millions flow;
disorientated seed,
saved
to be sent spinning across space
in spirals
of potential lost;
free to be trapped to be counted:

eight,
ironically;
only impotency;
others left to tip the balance,
although,
in essence,
only one is needed
to continue the wavering line
of vanity.

two girls on a worn doorstep

still smiling despite;

still smiling
          five years on
          from being born
          beneath the sun
          onto Bolivian soil,

          an unsafe,
          tear-sodden,
                    sun-baked soil;

still waiting,
     sitting,
     unknowing of their father's
                         fate;

still missing;
          a victim
          of the
          midnight
          knock.

June 15th

scream

broad-daylight
scream

contained

outer shell
rattling

glass-like

fragile essence
holding

so far

Forgotten Roots

Somewhere, where eyes still stare
at the hatted rain-dance being danced,
I watched you spiral across the sodden sand
while a drum repeated its relentlessly rapid rhythm,
each beat sending you deeper into frenzy,
your limbs flaying, your head spinning,
oblivious to the tide mounting the shore....

Out at sea dolphins arched and plunged,
playing with the currents,
mirroring each movement you made, mockingly,
their wide smiles, like those of grotesque imbeciles,
sharing a private, aquatic, lunatic joke....

Your dream was to have found the eternal steps
that would have led you back to your forgotten roots,
back to where your mask was of rainbow scales,
each as perfect as the dream itself,
but someone, somewhere, where eyes still stare,
forgot to tell you, as you rushed to dance,
that the sun could shine once only before dying....

And that, inevitably, was the joke they shared,
cruelly and at your expense,
though, oblivious as you were to the mounting tide,
you were equally so to this derision, as though
nothing mattered but your search for forgotten roots.

Lewis

everything new,
worth a look;

his eyes size up
the situation
with a one-hand-clapping
contemplation;

every colour,
every shape,
fresh,
unseen,
virgin,

each to be taken in,
to be used,
to become accustomed to,
to be lived;

an entire future stretches out
in front,
and he reaches,
with, as yet, uncoordinated arms,
to touch it,
to hold it,
to grow.....

Bourock 61/89

.... And where it all began is now blackened sandstone
poking fun at the heavens from amidst a wilderness
of empty space, razed monuments to home and work;

The heart has been drawn
to leave only the surrounding flesh;

Yet, another heart, though not wanting to be there,
still beats in sympathy with the pulse that surrounded it
when its world was new and small and warm;

But even that time, now,
seems to belong to a fading, browning past;

So much water has passed beneath the bridge's arch
as to make any thought of return a stupidity of mood,
a nonsense wrapped in sentimentality's smothering shroud;

Though, despite this, even time
in passing fails to obliterate everything;

The sandstone may be blackened, but perhaps it was
blackened to begin with and, quite simply, was never
noticed as being anything other than the sandstone it is;

Perhaps it is only now, from so far away,
that it becomes easier to see the filth....

Anonymous

In time-torn hands he holds all, his everything,
his summers' dreams and winters' hopes,
as though cupping a butterfly
of whose escape he is afraid;
unfulfilled, abstract, these memories eventually
to be taken below into the darkness of the sod.

In the meantime, the silence he knows is as ever,
surrounding, suffocating;
every street and doorway echoes with nothingness;
and, amidst it, he struggles to find
the feelings he was born to feel;
remote emotions now barely remembered.

He bends to pick up a discarded yet smouldering
cigarette butt
only to discover within it a symbol of himself.

And, like a clown's, his shoes
are different sizes , different colours,
his coat a patchwork of miles,
his trousers straining to retain
a seemingly unnecessary modesty;
but this clown makes no-one laugh;
to most he is invisible,
exiled by blind-eyed time.

He seeks warmth where the linoleum is cracked
and ancient wood supports the daily news;
he talks to the chairs, patting them
with a paternalism unable to be channelled elsewhere;
he peers at the newspapers with only an inch
separating his nose from the print;
yet, what part does he (indeed do any of us) play
in this history of events?

He is no-one, an anonym, innominate,
with brothers and sisters equally unknown, unseen,
invisible,
part of a family with no home and no roots;
he is as free yet as caged as a bird;

he is himself,
he is me,
he is you,
each of us cupping a butterfly between our hands
and struggling to feel, struggling to be seen by time.

Found dead,
unheard in parting,
with his frozen limbs spread in crucifix;
an unrecognized martyr denied martyrdom;
his summers' dreams and winters' hopes
ready to be taken below,
ready to be wrapped in smothering soil;
his part finally played,
his obituary an unwritten thought.

amalgam

though spartan as a whole
                    each note
                    (forced onward
                                outward
                    by pursed lips
                                caressing reed)
                    drips from the brassed bell
                    with an innate emotion
        lacing the arpeggio's birth

then cadenza
        spiralling
        spitting in sound
            the vision held
                    behind closed eyes
                            (cloistered image
                                    from childhood
                    or from upon the linen
                    of the night before)

            the spartanism
            submits
        to a rotundity
    and fullness
promising an interminability
                    that no promise
                        could ever hope
                        nor be held
                                to fulfill

scenario

    his room,
    his space,
    his world,
      is indistinct,
      monochromatic...

      his face,
      expressionless
    and out of focus,
    watches us
    watching him...

      his eyes
are so slow to blink...

      his mouth
        is wordless,
        still,
        silent...

but in the air
there are voices
      chanting
something similar
to the eternal .....

    and we,
      as spectators,
are forced to realize
that he is, as we are,
        here and now...

Zen Ghosts

the further I look, the less I see,
the less I see, the further I look,
and,
all in all,
there is so little to be seen
beyond these eight walls
where, within,
we,
lovers once and lovers still,
haunt the hours of our own captivity:

with hands held
and holding each other
we pass the time waiting for tomorrow,
looking ever further
but still seeing so little,
pinning hopeless hopes
to the air
as though expecting the space to be filled by
something solid,
something touching to be
touched:

the further you look, the less I see,
the less you see, the further I look,
and,
all in all,
together, we are ghosts of our own beliefs,
ghosts caught in the flow,
struggling
to remain above the surface,
struggling
to retain the key
to each dawn.

Indiscriminate

Somehow,
this ferocious game,
once started,
refuses to be stopped,
to die,
obstinately insane,
flying alone
like starved summer shadows
of a struggling world
where everything ends
with nothing understood:

This ruse
is without an answer,
without a face,
nameless;

To ask the question
is to feel the cold -

*

I have watched,
wanting to see mercy,
and have spoken words
that were never wanted...

I have offered an answer
that was simply a question
too soon to be asked,
too absurd to be clear;

But each hour
must have its pains,
each must wake at dawn -

*

Yet,
until such an awakening,
the sky must darken

with blood-red shadows
if the moments
are to crumble,
if these gathered hours
of waiting for the dream-eye to open,
of waiting for it to expose
the dreams dreamt
beneath its closed lid,
are to be laid bare,
carcass-like,
with every wart,
every blemish
as apparent as
the snarling of the game...
its ferocity unmatchable,
unstoppable,
unthinkably frenzied...
its faceless face
and bodiless body
spattered with the sweat
of the herd who have tried,
foolhardily,
to keep up,
the mustering who mutter *must*
with such breathless sincerity
as to make the *must*
a must
if it is heard at all...

'The sky *must* darken...'

'Each *must* wake at dawn...'

So much has become imperative
that the options have been slimmed;
(slim chance,
slim hope)
and there's no-one's
hand to hold,
no-one's
eyes to share a glance,
no-one's
breath to feel upon flesh
as felt before

when the whispers
of soft spillage
went unheard:

I have watched it all
and have spoken words
that were never wanted -

*

I have heard
each and every
of my kith's
struggling gasps
as they spend these hours
fighting to keep their heads
above the surface
of the consuming current
with its unseen undertow
always threatening,
always indiscriminate
in choosing the next
to be dragged down
towards a silent death:

I have heard them,
but have remained
unable to aid;
my own part in this,
as much as any other,
is one of being tied,
of being bound to the battle
that involves no other;
these hours, being born
from solitude's womb,
are forever
as solitude's fruit -

*

'Each hour
must have its pains...'
and each pain
must be acknowledged

if the painlessness
of other hours
is to be sensed:

Each pain's presence
must be admitted to
if the awakening
is ever to arrive
and the moments
are, at last, to crumble,
dust-like -

*

And,
though the riddle,
the answerless question,
continues to thrash,
there are brief seconds
when a mirror,
showing my own face,
can be seen:

The agonized expression
(drawn and haggard
by time)
is barely recognizable,
hardly familiar,
as though belonging
to someone
other than myself:

But it *is* my face,
the expression
one of one
in mid-flow
of following
in the hope that the ferocity
can be overcome
or will die its own peculiar death:

Though, somehow,
this game, once started,
refuses to be stopped,

to die,
obstinately insane,
flying alone...

* *

Castles of Sand

So slowly
it all turns to dust
to be blown
along the shore
where the land
meets the sea
and each moment
is fragile

Two lovers
hand in hand
walk against
the storm
their eyes
closed to the dust
unwilling to witness
its passing

But they as we as I
are a part
of the crumbling
of all we have built
always ignoring
the sun
and the reason
for its shadows

They as we as I
belong to the dust
to the storm
to the shore
blissfully blind
to the fragility
of the moment
and beyond

poem from the gut

no-one asked,
no-one said, "would you mind?",
reckoned it was fine
just to go ahead,
    to do it,
    to draw blood
        as though the anaemia
        wouldn't kill,
        as though the imbalance
                    of the scales
            wouldn't be noticed;

    but it was;

and the only ones left
with their heads
        buried up their arses
        were the ones
            who didn't ask,
            who should've asked,
            who should've stopped
        to think
before piercing the flesh,
        an act that
        put a number on their days;

    a suicide of sorts.

Genealogy - F.V. Berghe

With eyes eclipsed by Elysium's shade,
they visited, uninvited,
each an ancestor,
each stripped bare
as though nakedness was a medal,
the laurels won in honourable death,
in a hero's departure:

Behind them, their womenfolk and children,
equally sightless in the brightness,
unequally upright,
straight-backed,
erect,
waited, unburdened by the weight
of heroism remembered:

Before them, I sat,
with the gulf of generations between us,
expecting their cavernous mouths
to fill with words of warning,
or of reprimand,
but all that was heard
were the wings of a butterfly passing.

Sutton Bank

We looked into the sky,
hoping it would reveal even the slightest of hints,
the smallest clue to the cause of the fire
that burnt within us;
a common fire;
its flames equally shared, equally felt
as we waited for the darkness
of our own mortality to fall:

And, in that sky, a swooping swallow flew,
as though seeking our attention,
as though awaiting the moment
to deliver its message,
to tell us the secret
it had been sent to tell;
but it passed in silence,
wanting only to be seen:

We watched the sky
as the trespassing halo of the city beyond
ravaged the clouds with its jaundiced light;
we were strangers to its source,
strangers to the streets and alleyways,
strangers to the ways of those
who lived within the sprawl
with nothing of the fire to be felt:

Where you and I stood,
we could sense the expanse of sod
radiating from beneath our feet,
stretching endlessly
as though to feed the fire we knew;
and we could smell the roots
that held our world together,
a world of solitude shared.

Swan-Song

From through this decade-long dishonesty
            of clinging on, of expecting something,
                  sometime, to break free and shatter
            these near-breadless years of restraint,
                  I, at last, begin to hear the swan-song;

My swan-song, sung for you:

You, you have given me everything
            of the nothing you have for giving,
                  you have forgotten the simple syllables
                        it takes to say either yes or no,
                  preferring, instead, to leave me hung;

But my neck has begun to ache:

You have shown me how easily
                  you can become a thief of thoughts
                        and how much of an obstacle
                        can be made of your conceit,
            though, quite what you have to be proud of....

Maybe this enigma is your saviour:

You have provided me with dreams
                  and then turned them to nightmares,
                  delirious hours of being strangled
                        by the thinnest of ruby ribbons
                        that cut at my bleeding flesh;

Flesh that crawls with this air's stench:

You have slowly suffocated me
                  with your unashamed, unsensed apathy,
                  an artless apathy that wants what it knows,
                        yet doesn't know what it wants
                  beyond the certainty of well-oiled nights;

Nights laced with perfume and puke:

Tell me I am being unfair in thinking
                of you in such a roseless light,
        but only tell me if you have failed to see
    anything of yourself in these poisoned letters,
        a poison for which I make no excuses;

I am willing to concede, but not to stay:

You have twice already twisted my brain,
        to remain for a third would be simply insane,
    a madness through which I will not spectate
    as you have spectated from the safety of numbers,
        from the smugness of a self-bolstered past;

Though, the only history you have is false:

And now, now is too late to offer me olives,
        too late to persuade me to try any more,
            too late to expect me to die each
        of the thousand deaths already died
        over again for the sake of your whims;

The only death I want is of memories:

Still, no doubt, you will haunt me for longer
            than the length of the nights I have spent
    listening to your sleepless streets' endless echoes,
            but, if your haunting is to win my soul,
        that, you will find, has already been lost;

Destroying the destroyed is a fruitless cause:

Yet, such causes were always yours,
        watching for rainbows and lining your rooms
                and your hours and your minds
            with the worthlessly tacky trophies
            such sedentary pursuits provide;

Though, what I wanted to leave you was gold.

soulless death

stagnancy

a dead sea
a thoughtless mind

a nothingness
that holds none
of the promised beauty

blocked

over-familiar
unfriendly

every face and street
and sound and smell
well-known

no-one

nobody
nothing

the blandness begs
to be otherwise
but brings the decay

dead

a dead soul
a soulless death

No, Don't Fuck Off
Back To Israel

Your snake-hiss words
render this space,
these faces,
your audience,
silent,
respectful in their quietude,
keen to catch
every syllable,
every assonance,
every image you have come,
willingly,
to squeeze into their minds:

For part of the caress
of hands across
time's blank face,
you become a demi-god,
deified,
held in awe.

for J.S.

Complete

At last
   the trumpet
and broken chains,

 a gull in flight
flies now on its own,

       heralded,

    the ring of brass
becoming a roar
  of voices,

  desperate to tell,
       to state,
       to send the gull
           on its way,

   heavenward,

with a future,
   a place.

Apart

At last
the hour
of this loneliness
arrives
with the silence
grabbing
at my ears
and this space
we call home
again too large
for one
as it is always
too small
for two.

And your
departure
although for only
the time
of one
night-sun's path
pierces
the chrysalid
comfort
of having
you here
to hear
my jesterish
sighs.

As the hour
becomes hours
then days
each
will be counted
with childish
impatience
each
will be scored
in tally
as though

by a prisoner
upon an echoing
dungeon wall.

From Here

From here, amidst the grey,
      I wonder if the ocean in your eyes
      is ebbing or flowing,
      and whether the starling
      that wakes you each morning
      is the same as that
      which eases me, with its song,
      into the silence of evening.

From here,
      I wonder if, in looking
      up to where the night-sun shines,
      I will see your face
      within its round,
      and whether, upon your cheek,
      I will see loneliness trace
      a salted path.

From here,
      I wonder if the warmth of your smile
      is as warm as when
      those smiles are for me,
      and whether your voice
      is as soft
      as when your words are spoken
      in our sun-set hours.

From here,
      the distance between us
      is so great as to make
      wondering my only way
      of passing these empty hours
      as I lie, wrapped and alone
      in the coldest
      of linen cocoons.

August Fragments

She could see the air, still enough to be dead,
dead enough to have roared
like sandflies kissing stone,
and all around her were whispering, gathering birds,
savage in the moonlight, possessed by blood.

Air,
stone,
blood,

these, to her, were the exquisite victims
of the night,
her night,
moist and warm to be felt, to the face, to her.

I asked her name, but she explained
that to have one was as belonging,
a stifling belonging.

She wanted, simply, to be,
nothing more.

Only then could I see that, savage as they were,
the gathering birds were but ghosts of her past,
poisoned by time, possessed by blood.

She spoke to each of skin and bones,
as if anticipating the sun.

She spoke to each of the dust they would come to be.

I watched as she cut her fear
to a handful of trust,
careful not to make a noise,
frightened by her flow of wet, yet welcome, blessings.

Like flowers, each was a song of love,
of thankful reflection;
each was beauty
enclosed in the skin of the remembered dead,
her remembered ghosts.

Skin,
bones,
dust,

these, to her, were the fuel
of the silent lizards of time,
her time,
poisoned,
raped by the moon.

But, she refused the morning,
clearly lost in her expressionless
procession of thought,
confined to the night.
Her mysterious work had a pointlessness
that, for me, turned the moonlight black.

And, so, as she continued with her blessings,
I faded back into the shadows,
unnoticed,
unneeded,
but with her image and her words
still clinging to my mind.

From somewhere above,
I heard the weary hoot of an owl
seemingly tired of wisdom,
wistful in its song.

I could sense its need for simplicity
much as I could sense my own.

Coming upon a stream, I stood at its edge,
listening to it sigh to be as great as an ocean.

Along its borders were the rounded pebbles
of unknown time,
tiny beached whales with memories longer than my own.

I stooped to lift one in my hand,
to feel its smoothness,
to discover what it knew of before.

But, all it knew was how easily the soul can fall foul
of the Siren's call,
and how easily, once fallen, such a soul
can throw itself, prostrate,
upon the ashes of repentance.

I pocketed that stone as a reminder of my sins,
the ghosts of my own past.

As I looked up from this reverie, I saw,
standing upon the opposite bank,
a man without a face,
smiling with lips he did not have,
watching with eyes he did not have,
talking with a tongue he did not have.

"Stranger, I have watched you feel the smoothness
of the pebble you have taken from this stream,
and I have watched you question your past,
but let me tell you of mine that you may learn....

"I, too, have trapsed, as you have,
with gnawing isolation as my only companion,
and I, like you, have sought simplicity
yet found only the nauseous, intestinal tangle
of this world, each moment seemingly stained
by its own superfluous ontology....

"And, Stranger, I, too, have seen the Nameless Woman
who blesses the birds,
and have discerned only pointlessness.
Yet, I have learnt to walk and watch and see and hear
without to question.
I have learnt to empty my pockets of every pebble
I have ever kept to remind me of my sins,
for, if anything,
I have discovered sin to be only momentary."

Then, with that said,
his facelessness became nothingness
as he left me, once again, alone,
my mind choking on his words as it tried to make sense,
to learn,
to understand,

to take what he had said and mould it into action,
into will.

In being alone, I thought again of the Nameless Woman
who, in my thoughts, had become more than skin and bones,
more than air and blood.

The Siren she was
gave way to an eternal ebbing and flowing,
for she had become as the stream had wished to be;
an ocean in which thoughts were secret.

And, in her fathomless being, I began to see
something of myself, if only distorted reflections;

my need of love,
of trust,
of tenderness,
of the warmth
of another,
of knowing the nest to be full.

Yet, in meeting these then, they were as never before,
felt as though for the first time.

But, in returning to where she had been,
I found only an unquestionable silence
in which not even a feather stirred.

Alone in the sky,
the sun had begun upon its ritual path.

between

momentary stagnancy

starched
still

soundless

stretching endlessly
in waiting

willing

ready to move
on this tide

this time

Weighing

With this alone,
with this passing sweep
of hands across figured ivory,
there remains
but one act to perform:
to count the apples on the trees,
both ripe and rotten,
measuring each against the other
as though to finally find
the weight of gold.

Towards an Awaited Exorcism

Along these shores
a new life opens its wings
and begins its flight
across an unknown familiarity
where my own unborn past
has lived and died
in the innumerable names
and faces of unending years,
every one of which
holds a story to be told again.

Such soaring is, perhaps, indulgence,
yet deserved after so long
spent with feathers clipped
by the hand of deprivation
that knew no limits
in its love of torture,
itself justifiable only
in being believed to be love
for which all was sufferable
until the suffering stung.

Such soaring opens out
the garden of hissing tongues
into acres of liberty
where the hissing becomes a song
sung by voices with compassion
handed down through generations
that have known grief,
known strife for what it is
and where it leads
when, for each, the day has ended.

And this could be
the top of the world, as promised,
as a heaven amongst laughter
for which cure is unsought,
unwanted, unnecessary in hours
that have shaken off the ties
of assertions built upon myths,
mighty myths that bring

all in their path to stagnancy
born of unbridled pride.

Here, too, I begin to shake off
the sod-hugging realities
of the indifference of others
and of their greed,
both of these having clipped
even my wings for so long,
even mine, wings that once
bore me on a flight
that threatened no return,
no escape, whether right or wrong.

This flight, though, is different;
there is the taste of escape
in the air that fills me
and which I return to its whole
with so little taken from it
but a hopefulness,
a simple, forgotten optimism,
a faith heaving with dawns
as countless as the smiles
upon lovers' lips:

There is the sight
of unending, unvanquishable horizons
which, despite my desire
to return to the cloisters of the womb,
fill the scope of my eyes
with a security never before
felt as it is felt now,
carefree and belly-full,
content but far from complacent,
closer to complete.

Yet this completion, of sorts,
will only ever be as close
as to be a shoulder-rubbing reality
when the grasping remnant
of the unforgettable nightmare
is finally severed
and the colour of its blood is seen,
if, indeed, blood it has,

for such a warmth
has never been its to boast of.

And so, although this could be
the top of the world, as promised,
I am forced to wait longer still,
soaring in an uncertainty
which, unwittingly, torments me,
making my feathers falter
in keeping me aloft,
above and along these shores
where the sands shift
as has always, irreversibly been meant.

Sandy

From myrtle to thorn,
though never quite sure
if it was too late
or of no effect
in the turning of the screw
that made a martyr;

Whichever, the move
belonged solely to him,
the man who I have always
wanted to meet in person,
but met only in anecdote
and with infant's eyes;

In myrtle, he passed
me the generation
that made my own,
in thorn, he died
his gasping death
between walnut boards.

Cleansed

While the moon swallows
what's left of the taste of day,
the roar of the rush relaxes,
becoming only a passing
timed by the changing
of red to green.

These, coming from outside,
are new sounds,
as unfamiliar as those, from inside,
of the creak of wood
and the settling
of a century's stone and slate.

But this, after all, above all else,
is why I have come,
why I am here,
breathing greedily
as my senses are cleansed
of a contempt born of time.

In the Fragility

This flower
opens its petals
        to spit,
and I am lost,
reduced to a shadow
    cast upon the earth,
            directionless
    and without dimension,
a song unsung,
a history untold:

    My voice,
    as it flows
        as an inky stream
of allusions,
    falls on ears
attuned only
        to the rustle
of regal-faced leaves
            brought upon the winds
of other men's Autumns:

And yet, in this,
            here, somewhere between
    my Spring and so slowly
unfolding Summer,
        there begins and ends
            all of that which,
                in short,
is my own notion
of a raison d'être,
a life-line in the fragility.

Empathies

Stubble-faced fields
stretch upon sweeping waves
of the centuries' passing,
leading downward,
seaward,
from the heaven
of now-dead, sunken hopes
to the water-worn, wooden pillars
of a previous prosperity
in which afar came nearer
to remain only in name.

From these acres
and forming fathoms
there rises the ghost
of an ageless age,
timeless times,
still held dear in hearts
too afraid
to focus on an aimless tomorrow,
a future
laced with further failure
and empty hours.

From this heavy earth
and restless water
there is evoked a feeling
of unending uncertainty,
of transience too overwhelming
to risk being spoken of
in anything other
than voices
that would otherwise
be reserved
for the night.

And, yet, it is here
that I find
my ancient brethren,
feel their familiar fear
and share my past

with their future
as though twins separated
by a singular,
though critical, moment
while immersed in the angst
of birth.

It is here
that the circle of coincidence
is finally tied,
end to end,
in a completion
to span generations
of empty-hearted wandering,
to welcome the ghost,
for myself,
with outstretched arms
and a smile.

stubborn

slow-eyed dawn

      dreaming
      still

  a half-lit
    half-way world

ringing

resonant

reluctant to cede
    to the swelling sun

    unwilling to allow
the chorus to begin

pricked with rain

the sky's tides
break upon
these streets' shores

heavily

hungrily
devouring all evidence
of the morning's sun

the sun beneath which
a child had asked
whether the vividness
of his dreams
was matched by my own

the question
seemingly innocent

at the time

this dampness
only now
giving it an edge

as to cut

to pierce

thorny in the flesh
of these cold-grown hours

each a dulled
reflection of time

of age

of when

wind-swept

growing cold

      the wind wakes
and thoughts are scattered

no sense

no single pin-point
remains long enough
   to be considered

  to be honed

     sharpened
     to conclusion

only this blur
of signals

uncoded

unsorted

     the space to focus
        denied

the luxury of shelter
unfound

sixth hour

sun
drops

dry

whispers
heard

faint
yet piercing
with meaning

much needed

awaited

prophet's sighs
disguised

dusk's echoes
replete
with allusive
quiescence

struggling

the hours between
womb and grave
mirrored
in the crawl
up Clinkum Brae

horses straining

guzzling
the sand-scented blood
of a distant war

the ascent
a murderer
in a different form

a killer
without remorse
who gives minutes
a razor-sharpness

filling each
with breathlessness
and regret

primal

finger-tips itch
for the touch
of earth
while the heart
belonging
drowns
in sterile waters
of invention
surfaced
to a lie
of perfection

in the process

embellishing skin
drawn back

bones of words
bared

and begun
again
this process
of searching

of doubting

of making
skeletal sense
of obese thoughts

of laying
old ghosts to rest

for a while
at least

until dragged out
with a change
of wind

direction unknown

first light

brewing dawn
aloft

robed
to receive
its solemn name

accompanied
by the pious chatter
and chanting
of many tongues

each strengthened
by this morning ritual

this day
inherited
from a silhouetted world

vacuum

in uncertain hands
the rust crumbles

fragile with age

leaving only
a dust-pile

growing
with every
dungless moment

filling out

swelling
to become
fallow acres
of mounting fragments

scraps of living

past snatches
of a world perceived

sensed

taken
piecemeal
from a context
too overwhelming
to be taken whole

too complex

too immense
for the brevity it allows
to become anything other
than rust

crumbling

held by
doubt

in toto

a lashing
lizard's tongue
breaks the air

and the surrounding
silence
is strangled
into a screaming
submission

effortlessly

as though
the intrusion
was expected

invited

welcomed
in toto
as the hour's
inevitable course

harsh realities

skin
against skin

prayers end

sins collide

created
acquitted

together

then
stolid echoes
of murmuring

a final phrase
detached

unaffected
by the brutality

by the razing
of hopes

enshrined

innately innocent

instinctively formed
only
to be
crushed

menses over

tearing
at shadows

moon eyes

moping

soured
by years

yet
watchful as ever

patient as ever

primed
with kindness
found in age

bound by instinct
to each growing reflection

piperpool

wind-blown time
in white
wakes in the carrying
of its soul
across sunday acres
to dance the steps
of a formless dancer
neither seen
nor heard
known of only
in the rook-filled sky's
fading falling fire

meanwhile

a stale whisper
of broken promises
surfaces
as the sun is searched
for a reflection
of the mighty whale
which
as ever
is not life....

.... all in a day in a game
of infinite floundering

a game in which
the day has no name
other than sometime

sometime soon

sometime
to suit such whims
as are revered
and rewarded
behind closed doors....

.... meanwhile
another slave suffers
on the cross

the cracking of skulls

tides crawl
as ever
so slowly
to mark
the beginnings
and endings

the cracking of skulls

though
only a madman
would kiss
goodnight
to the stars

Crossing

Beyond the wave-sprayed glass
of these six or so hours,
there is the passage of a watery
no-man's land
that lies, as ever, exposed to the horizon,
its surface barren, yet carrying
all upon it as though within a womb,
softly swelling, faintly falling,
curiously comforting,
despite the unknowing.

taught to kill

these aesthetic waters,
already tasted,

poisoned;

preconceptions carried
without even so much
as a second, lateral glance:

already tasted;

the taste, one of oil
for smoothing the great machine
along its faceless track,

mechanisms rumbling,
yet making nothing,

idling,

turning for the sake of turning
in circles of pointless importance:

already tasted,

now shunned,

spat out
at every opportunity;

the shifting edge,
the moving target:

pleasure eroded;

the message implicit
in unraised spastic hands
and eyes filled with loathing:

already tasted;

already dead.

So Far Forever

Always a minute more than when

defiantly so

as though
to make a mockery of every now
never quite

night after day after night

forever and
always

Moving On

Moving in
slowly
under a heron's gaze
to submerge the summer

the tide
makes its mark

advancing
to obscure
every trace
of barefoot tracks
across the sand.

Cormorants
and guillemots
take to the highground
of the outcrops

and
like you
I begin to feel the chill
of knowing
our freedom to be fading.

Simplification

In retrospect

now
so seemingly sightless

to the point
where
a dead seagull
would be only that.

Fraternity

From where we are
where we were
takes until dawn to rest;

a slow crucifixion
in a rare mastication
of siblings' cud.

Cigarette

As yet another tower of ash
tumbles to the floor,
time is marked by the silence
of its scattering
in the cold-chill draught of solitude.

pointless act

nothing
    is sacred
nothing
    is safe

dreams gone
    dust bitten

    class
   war
      own
     goal

on time

I

nearing home
in a blend of found thoughts
and painted eyes

of darkening heavens
and only one laugh

too quiet a laugh to matter

too soon to fear the future
as if it had been heard of
in a discarded word

another time
let slip

II

a sigh
then caresses

the past deserted
neglected

more than ever
known of only as dead and gone

III

your hands
welcome me

your mouth
silent

only one laugh
mine

too quiet to be thought of
as anything other
than the present
awake

74

Parallels left across stubbled acres
become again unseen
until the scarlet spits,
unceremoniously,
as a staccato in the silence,
a reminder in the forgetfulness
of this unrelenting haste.

Sutherland

From between folded hills
an eye stares out
in recrimination,
damning the dawn
for the first fuck it forgot,
spewing yellow,
suicidal,
while the sky
becomes bloodied
by expectancy:

And your part
in all of this
is that of an aesthete
perched on one peak
in reflection,
reflecting upon the value
of vision.

Last Gasp

Blood comes pouring
from a skinned tree;

the place immaterial;

the end memorable
for the disbelief
incited by this death.

Cracked

I have said my piece
and no longer want to speak;
muteness, like a swan's.

Static/Stagnant

Rising,
falling,
a fresh-furrowed ocean
of earthy waves
teases the hills
into joining its game
of calling in echo
to the cormorants' cries:

While,
for you and I,
the game is one
of moving on
in avoidance of the curse
that makes open eyes
no different
from closed.

Like Home

You take me,
with every tenderness,
into your arms
and call me
by the name of the child
you haven't yet had.

Machrie Water

As sibling shadows
climb across the scarred stone
and velvet green of A'Chruach,
dusk makes its presence
felt all the more,
threatening night and its darkness
through which only the Machrie Water
will continue to flow.

Trauma

Amidst the same stones
that once witnessed
the making of a dead-man
of the father
of my mother,
we scramble, clamber,
caught up in a crab-like,
crawling, clawing trinity
in which facelessness
binds each part to the whole.

Refusing to relinquish,
to even slacken its hold,
our fatigued senses
become its tight-held prey,
while all around us,
so long so solid,
turns soft as sodden soil,
saturated earth,
barren, lifeless,
its future in doubt.

This trinity is complete
in being endless,
timelessly immortal,
while we, slowly suffocating,
face an extinction
that is only ever recorded
in engraved petrification,
yet we continue to scramble,
clamber, struggle to be free
to draw breath in the wind.

Into the Hills

At last,
hyena;

wounds licked.

To Talk

Somehow, suddenly, it is as though
you had never known how to speak,
your reticence having gestated
upon a different tongue;
different circumstances;
another language,
crippled with dull-buffed edges:

but, still, you are able to do this;
to talk to yourself,
to talk with clarity,
to talk.

Prayer

As the murmured words
become warmer,
leaner,
their tonal totality,
in all its sinuosity,
becomes oppressive,
as if downhill,

while the timetable
of timelessness,
a gannet
to piscine minutes and hours,
shatters under the weight
of its own recondite syntax,
steaming as it splinters and dies.

Tough Shit

As though eyes would reach the ground,
there were two sides to speak,
to spear the silent, empty air
with time, broken beneath the darkness,
pushing to bridge this and the next
of a tongue brought from the black,
brought from a numbed dream.

The ocean could have shed the mark
of the sudden dance of mock hours,
but, between the caressing sun of morning
and the brooding voice of nightmare,
it could only split the sound of croaking ash,
twitching in a long hiss of whispering wind
full of meaning and, yet, meaning nothing.

Eyes, ocean, nothing; silence with teeth:
this focused energy, gathering blood and fire,
had gnawed away at our tangled panic
before we could hunt for the ritual words,
never stopping, never standing to pause in time,
its restlessness staining the tide of the sky
with the near-inaudible sounds of a demented world.

Retreaded

I have followed you so long
towards your own form of chaos:
it is only now I see my reflection,
complete with domino;
an unknown, unrecognizable face.

My own amalgam of history and future
I understand and begin to remember;
deeply uncomplicated,
uncomplicatedly deep.

Though, I will not wave you any farewell;
you are not gone, nor will you go:
we are inextricably linked
in a paradoxically simple imbroglio
by the common water and air
that give us life;
here, now, always.

making statements

you are

still screaming about
who it's at
what it's at
where it's at
why it's at
when it's at
and are still missing the point

you are

from three paintings
by rupert m. loydell

I.

alone
despite the fullness
the trinity

a capacity
for all to be one

for this one
to be fore
and be four

solid
amidst sea

II.

we are
complete

no end
no beginning

while
we stand
side by side
with the boles
that bridge
yesterday
and tomorrow

blue light
permeating
the holt

III.

by day
through night

in youth
then age

parallel lives

shared faith

Moving On

In progression,
the sun breaks free
from the collusion of chattering clouds
with only whispered vespers
to separate it from the way
that glares with echoed hues of rape
towards other hours:

yet, this circle is not of fire;

more of coincidences
that make a never being
of having gone;
of having lived with a single name
through several lives
that come, eventually, to be one:

and I, meanwhile, grow older still,
older than immodest stars
that bark and belch and blow their horns;

I move without moving,
finding that generations never really die,
lying, instead, in wait
as arrows of sand amongst the grass
beneath the emptiness
of where the sun once passed
on its steady path, now
in progression.

where it's leading

little
   more
      than
       stutters

      scattered
impenetrability

as always

as calm
as naked bones

perhaps

the idea
that just when
each breath became
a stammered word
each minute would
have been already enough
finally made sense

though the calm remained
only as perhaps

as always
as naked bones

Out of the Rut

When the gulls
turn their backs
on the sea
for the worm,

time
for change;

the season
for ploughing up
the present,

for exposing
the fecundity
of possibilities
denied
for so long
for the sake
of hopes
and second chances;

precisely the moment
for moving on,

for foraging
in the furrows
of an earthy,
earthly uncertainty:

no more minutes
to fill
to hours
of clutching
at final straws
and growing
long in the tooth;

no more hours
to fill
to days
of pissing

in the wind
and praying for escape;

no more days
to fill
to weeks....

Time to turn, too,
from the sea.

hunger

to an end
already

pressed against
invented luck
with nothing to do

while
unbelievably
no peace

whatever more
curiously possible

anything

*

actions

emotion

in this
final insanity
nothing else
is said

*

no name

as yet

eight weeks

already you are
eyes
ears
and a beating heart

part of me
and of she
who have waited so long
to name you

4.5cm

in there
you
waiting
growing

there
where elsewhere
I would like
still to be

Heard Like Blood

In our broken thinking, as if you had found
that to laugh was to hide from pain and time
and I that in every stream nothing but patience
was to be felt, experienced and kept so long;
in such thinking, where pleasure and perplexity
                              walked arm in arm,
where once there had been the strangest sadness,
there now were so many blindly silent eyes.

No words, never words, never replies: this new madness
was crawled into, as if into a garden remembered
only for the shadow it had awakened, like secrets
understood by no mind but that of man from boy;
and, once crawled into, you and I, together,
were to come to be a gnawing hunger
for a voice along the river this sorrow had left.

You and I were to become the transitory flesh
of the dice player, so old, so ugly, yet smiling,
listened to by the hummingbird with mounting happiness;
and, at the same time, that of the child, so new, so loved,
                              yet, sure of nothing,
neither awake nor asleep, empty of all reason and folly:
you and I learned to be these and, by this path, finally
discovered a consciousness that is heard like blood.

returning

....until, in its time,
another dawn,
another day,
another chance
for this wordlessness to breathe
and search some sort of sense
amongst the darkly chaotic
of seed, subtle, small.

Versus

Any child, any number of years, anywhere,
now marks out my future, pin-pointing
ages, stages, in an imminent fatherhood,

and all I can do is look on, spectating,
wondering how all this sizes up against
long-held ideals borrowed from the east:

a solitary point between before and to come,
never there, always here, begins to become
a seed to be chased around within my mind.

Such doubt, perhaps, is an inevitability when
all else is in flux and the smallest strand
of stability is clutched at, white-knuckled;

such doubt, perhaps, is an inevitability when,
unnoticed, even the past in memories steals in
as a yardstick against which to reassess

every response and attitude, every value
and principle that so soon will be needed
and needed to be solid, unshakably held.

Though, conceivably, in such unmasked questions,
the answers are, themselves, somehow exposed
as the realities that are siblings to ideals;

that to understand what has already been
is to know today; that tomorrow will come
whether marked out by myself or child unknown;

and that, in doubt, when strong becomes weak,
weak, again, in turn, comes to be strong,
being one as the other, different only in name.

Further In

And yet more of having travelled,
of having learned
that the way of water
can change nothing
and that, on earth,
this world,
no words can carry
a sufficiency to know:

the hand may move
without its stillness being lost;

the poet may live
without the death of being heard.

Scan

In the half-light,
the nicotine glow
of sound in motion,
you watch me
as I watch the dawn
you cannot see,
though can feel within you,
within the stretching cave
where our dreams are made
that begins to fill with the
meaning of being;

to be
and continue so
through the others
of the magic,
the mystery
of our valley and loins,

no questions asked.

The Paradox of Pearls

He waves and is lost;
his beginning returns
to the foreknowledge
of old lives yet to linger,

as dew; he knows all

and still he knows nothing
to be shaped and polished
in the trap of an oyster,
to be spat and remembered
as an heirloom of words
for sometime, somewhere

down the line; simply empty

and, for this, all the more sad,
all the more scratched at and
battered by inadequacy,
all the less like flesh and blood
to be cherished, to be admired,

simply empty; no apology.

Dangerous

Now
the final ascent
begins;
so many of her words,
still,
seeking reassurance;
the hoping that all
will be well
in the end and beginning
yet to be heard
in the same struggled scream:

though, together, we know
so little of the workings
of miracles; so little,
then, at times,
seemingly,
so much,

too much.

Still

While she swells,
the moon's whispers
no longer hold any meaning
and what was
before we were
becomes so long ago.

The Relocation of Cerberus

Empty of all but focus, we wait;
each measured breath a wordless mist
into which our fingers draw a rising sun
that, so soon, will sere the flesh
of our every waking and sleeping hour;
a sun to which we will give a name
and fragments of our very own futures
beyond the time of the closing light.

And we, alone, will know of this sun
as other than only yet another,
knowing of its warmth as no others can,
filling each day with forgivable sentiment,
pardonable, if only for having tightly grasped
the chrysanthemums recalled elsewhere,
between white leaves spat upon by magi
who, as always, take no prisoners.

Meanwhile, we wait, empty of all but focus;
the wind, outside, howling round our memories,
collective and singular, shared and private;
there is little of this time left to us now
before we, ourselves, are given new names
as old as the original sin of the garden
where a childhood was scattered as tatters
with wreaths laid to mark the days.

We wait, the focus delivering its inertia
for us to breathe, talk and eat as starved
of breath, words and food with meaning;
only now does it start to come together
to form flowing waters, dark with purpose
drained as blood from the scars of battles
that, although history, hold our feet to the ground
as it turns without ever showing remorse.

The weight of this burden of patience tested
becomes a branded circle, empty yet full,
upon our ebbingly youthless skins,
stretching to accommodate the coming chaos
in which peace and turmoil will be ill-defined,

unlined, unseparated, unwilling to be known
as one without the other, unwilling to be held
in awe without having first been held in fear.

And when, in ignorance, I ask whether
the feeling is of congestion or of life,
your eyes reflect an unfathomable virtue
while your mouth returns the answer "both";
so complete a reminder of the whole
contained within the hollowness of time,
these days, this waiting and focus,
as to leave us strong again to embrace the dawn.

So?

and what of it
if this is all there is
this to and fro
and up and down
seemingly without purpose
except eventually
of reaching an end

Tactility

Maybe you're right:
maybe I have grown
to be out of touch,
maybe I am unable
to chant the mantras
of names and causes
as easily as before
anymore:
though, there again,
maybe it's just that
what I've come to touch
is less readily verbalized,
less to be acted upon,
more to be non-acted upon:
but is that to say
we can't both breathe
the same air, both
as it hangs around us
now
and as it is, itself,
laden with our past.

for J.C.

internal exile

then
beyond comrie
with every dawn
i put away
the distraction
of words
to absorb
the changing light
upon these distant hills

a silent ritual
as though to maintain
a fragile sanity

as though to hold
this illusion
within its context

repeated
repeated
time after time
while waiting

for the promised timelessness
the inevitable beinglessness
of after hours

doors locked
curtains closed

in requiem for another
earlier generation

though
from time to time
this altar afar
becomes a secret

invisible by birch here
or condensing vapour there

to tempt the lie
of out of sight
and therefore of mind

were it so easy

lifting

sun up
before even
the early bird
and at last
the grinding sadness
of winter
retreats

In Preparation

The need
to look back
before
moving on
becomes apparent
now

so much
blood
shed as
ink

so much
the virgin
stained

to what end

*

you can't help
but weep with
the uncertainty

floods
of homeless
worth

as though
it's all been
a case of
marking moments

of thoughts
of time

no real point

*

no reality
even
as you drag these
another three lines
down a page
to shore up
an again
faltering invention

conscious subject

self.

gone

the water
the air
the need

to move on

to diminish
time and dreams
to the reflected
imperfection
of actions

as drops
of possibility
bound in death

Await

Once again
the moment
has come
to dissect you

once more
to take
your opening
phrasing
and await
the storm
before the calm.

The final
drone
is where we
came in.

"Prayer for Peace"
Amalgam, 1969.

S/he

Within
and able
to perceive
so much
of what is to come

anytime

False Pretences

I was going
to gather flowers
but found
only barren acres

an authentic death

an end
with only
gathered belongings
again.

5.10

and you're talking
in my sleep

wanting to go
waters gone

life to come

family

she is the sea
through which
all life passes

while I am witness
to the vision
of all visions

of the sun
held aloft
and delivered

from she
into me

still smeared
with journey's blood

he
as yet
unaware of the day

May 1995